The Eddy Fence

P O E M S

by
Donna Henderson

Airlie
Press

Cover art "Black Rock" by Richard Bunse
Design by Cheryl McLean
Author photo by Richard Sutliff

PO Box 434
Monmouth, Oregon 97361
www.airliepress.org

ISBN 978-0-9821066-0-0
Library of Congress Control Number: 2008940511

Printed in the United States of America.

For Rich

Contents

*"If you did not look
what is it you 'loved'"*
—George Oppen, "Of Hours"

I

Triptych

I

In the dream I'd seen the way, like a painting, the poem could grow.
The poem feeling its way through dark, dab to dab, stroke
to stroke, note to corresponding note, to echo, each informed by the one
before, making at once the trail, its destination.

Pink ship in its little grove of shade.
The ship is painterly; a ridged, rose smudge against a grey smear,
syllable of vowels. A glow from the smudge, as from a setting
unseen sun. *Don't ask what the image means—look at it longer.*

Pure science, pure prayer: the same.
A way of investigation which seeks first and last to dissolve
each *a priori* until what's sought is seen.

Pink of the desert dusk on Eid, Jordan, 1999.
Blood from sheep slaughtered on rooftops
streams out of downspouts and through the streets.

||

The idea that I was all idea came to me, walking down to the mailbox.
That my substance itself was imagination, strenuous enough to gel,
persistent enough to continue. Inside of which substance
its source imagines also itself.

What was mine but desire to enter the world more entirely?
What's the self but these cuffs of self-consciousness,
entering's obstacle?

> *So much you want,*
so much less willing to bear—
And maybe the self's the vibration between these poles,
its material frequency and hum.

Outside, the ocean folds and falls, folds and
falls, crumbling to rills of light, the rills
scrambling up the sand. Three days of rain have turned the fields
to mirrors, here and there crisp tufts breaking through.

III

Dusk again. Finches—fat sparks—flitting through it.
A Swainson's thrush sings its haunted-house song in the distance,
its tune running up, over and over, the same four steps. The bird
sings from the woods, woods I'd assumed conferred its chambered,
spacious tune, song of a loneliness and the consolation

of loneliness; song from inside some still, dappled vastness
amid the trees. Then the bird flew to the clear-cut
and sang the same—
                    All these years I'd thought the thrush
sang from some spacious woods—!
The woods were in the song.

When I asked you your age

and you named it
(a little surprised: we'd been so
long without knowing),
your named age lay on my tongue like a lozenge,
curves and bars of your specific impermanence
tasting of roots and spice.

                    It was so intimate—
not the sum itself but the way it placed you,
love, between an end and a beginning…

And a delicate sadness started
making its rightful place with
joy as I stayed with this;
that my love had an age
and I knew it.

First Ice

We wake up as the darkness begins
giving way, first to an indigo

glow like laundry bluing,
phosphorescent and implausibly dense.

Shades of trees appear, then trees,
then a dreamy, scintillant

stillness unfurls as light, as landscape
under a spell. A fat sleekness

blisters and thickens the porch; in the pasture
grass blades bow down in glass sleeves.

The woods are themselves and not
themselves in their subtle glister,

the way a truly glamorous woman,
my grandmother used to say (charm bracelets rustling),

conceals every seam and trace
of her artifice, leaving pure effect.

Inside, a chef on T.V. makes aspic
while we wait for the forecast.

One strives for the clearest, thinnest
gel, he is saying; one wants to illuminate

one's terrine, not to thicken it!
And as he spreads his glaze, I see the soul

rise from its loaf and lay its glossy
immaterial bliss across that surface of meat &

salt with its scallion *fleur-de-lis*,
making it marvelous.

As the world is, today—as it was
in the beginning, that last instant

water, matter and light were one,
each distinct, not yet separate.

On Monastery Road

There are prayers on the corkboard,
pears on brown paper slabs

on the table a crowd of crumbs.
Outside a frog leaps

Basho-like into a pond.
Do I wish I were

elsewhere?
As usual,

though this is the elsewhere
I spent yesterday wishing for.

■ ■ ■

Beside the road a bitter mist hovers
over the fresh-killed fields.

The fields don't know they're dead,
the way they shine and sway

same as before the spray.
Bringing me to my senses, I say

to myself, then (pleased with this line),
the grasses teaching me how to live.

Except they aren't true, the lines;
they're my escape from the scary field.

To meaning, its "elsewhere."
There, that's truer.

■ ■ ■

This morning the moon has a hollow glow.
Glad to be barren (me too).

To Witness
(for J.M.)

You smoke alone on the precipice.
Below, fish slip visibly
down the long gullets of loons as wind
skitters across the river's surface
and disappears, to rise

tonight, by the fire
in the telling.

The Mole

Rounding a bend in the trail
down Neahkanie Mountain, a mole and I
startle each other.

Instantly I kick it,
startling myself.

Twice, to tell the whole truth.

A sharp chirp on the second kick
sticks like a burr,

more tenacious than excuses,
than the view from the summit,
that kick before thinking.

Easter Morning

All night rain spoke its spondees
into the grass and dust.

I rose, went to the window
to close it. Listening,

woke up and left it raised.

The Pasture

Then, perhaps on a certain night in June,
before I have given thought
to the idea of going down I just go

down,
to that edge where the pasture—dark
slope of my longing—
breaks from the cast light of the house,

and stand alone there.
The canyon uncaps its incense; dew and
dust and the knowledge of alders
rise to my aid.
Grass rustles to receive my ankles,
cats close in. The lit brook
sings from the copse, and the copse hums.

Not plunging forward, not turning back
toward the house, I simply
stay, and consent to suffer

the dark edge,
this gaze...

the abyss of beauty,
its two terrors:

that I could fall all the way into it.
And that it will not have me.

Between

It was a good garden, but I wanted it
moved from its plot uphill to the pond's edge

so I could work by the water—green glaze
shimmering away toward some distant willows—

and near the house a marsh
bridged the shift from dry to wet, erasing

seams, the ground going softer, then spongy, then
sunken but still visible through a crest of reeds

where cattle shambled hip-deep and ducks
churned; all the swimming and flying and walking things

met, it seemed to me, in that marsh,
grazing and gulping.

And I wanted to transplant my garden into that turgid soil
against all sense; to bury rootlets of kale, leeks,
squash among the muscular grasses, the wild seeds—

So I stood awhile like that, passing my hands
through the shallows, imagining the joy of whole days

kneeling between those solid and fluid worlds; all day
dipping and lifting.

View of Mt. St. Helens from the End of a Love Affair

Ten years later, I can't get
used to the mountain.

I come around the last curve and
there it is, each time half-
gone again. Then

the slap of loss again,
then pain like phantom limbs',
useless and intractable.

Anyone who'd never known the top
before it blew would see a summit:

broad and low, but still entire,
whole.
            I envy them that view—

no last few thousand feet of peak-shaped space,
no ghostly dotted lines containing it,

no presence of an absence I might love
if I could just remember it.

Standard Time
    (for Rod)

It was the day to reset the clocks.
I was fixing us lunch, you were dying from AIDS.
As I cooked you sipped Medoc *for the appetite,*
and sucked smoke *(why not?)* from a Gauloise.

It was April, this was Paris,
past the long, thin windows
plane trees were relaxing their grip on the first
green knots, and nimbus covered, then uncovered
the sun.

I was trying to recall which way to change
the clocks. *"Spring forward, fall back,"* I recited,
lifting a spoon. Then, your delight:
you'd never heard of this.
We Brits say "autumn," never "fall,"
you'd said; *our loss!*

We ate our meal in the new time, in silence.
Fever silvered the hollows and juts of your skull.
Across the rue de l'Eure a school bell blasted kids
loose to a yard where they milled and swirled—

            What's that you say? you keep on asking then,
            "Spring back, fall forward," isn't it?

Now when it's time to change I'm not sure
how it goes.

The Sanctuary

It was late when I walked up the gravel
road to the clear-cut hill. Loggers gone
for the day, feller-buncher machines all still,
their claws and blades cooling.
A low sun laid its thick light on the slope,
the light sieved through the last, lean stand.
Into those wrecked woods I walked,
straight to the center pile,
laid myself down on a log
and apologized for my species.

I apologized to those trees for my species
with tears, but not without greed:
I wanted a word in turn.
Of forgiveness, reassurance,
I don't know—I wanted a word.
Which didn't come.
And what was I thinking, wanting more?
The trees, after all, were dead.

The trees were dead—only the light was there;
which I saw (as I stood between the machines
and their gruesome business, amid the piles and vines)
coated the whole sorry mess of us all,
without chastisement or preference.

Without chastisement or preference, the light
left, and I walked back down that road
and up my own, home to a solitude I was
bereft of now, sullied as it was.
Woke the next day to watch, over again,
one fir after another lean to the left
and fall, keening and cracking (*Screamers*,
the painter Emily Carr had called them:
final splinters that shriek as the trunk is torn).
For so long—oh, *forever*—I had counted on the forest's
persistence there, its green and cool surround.
Not to escape the sufferings of the world:
from which to bear them.
Now the violence was taking the forest too,
while I stood on my cedar deck,
inconsolable, seeing unceasingly.

Inconsolable, seeing unceasingly
a word arrived through the wound—
       This is what it is to bear witness,
I saw inside. As the woods got small
the heart had to grow larger. To become,
by its breaking, what those woods had been.
Spacious, the heart would have to become,
and huge. Enough to hold all the trees
and their absence, and every other thing.

Blackberries

I

When we knew there would be no stopping it, in that year before the trees
went down, keening and cracking, when we knew

I turned away with my anguish, you went straight into those woods
with yours, into the still-tall, cool shade of their shelter and whispers

to see again, soak up their presence again toward the days of the absence,
again and again you went in, as you do and do.

And this two-years-later fall morning, the scabby shaved flesh of the slope
(seen for—what? The seven-hundredth-plus time?), its hundred-eight acres

I've yet to get used to (the thistles, the slash piles)—well, I wish
I had made myself go in there with you. Now I've neither the woods

nor their memory. *At least you have their memory* I said, *which is better.*
        I don't know if it is you said, looking away.

II

Lately it's been so hard to love this world, and no solace in nature—
        where's *nature?*

Not in the fields with their idiot fescue, its uniform grasses that passively
burgeon (too richly, too greenly) before turning orange from killer sprays.

In August the dust from the ruined soil swirls & swirls,
thickening the incessant-now dishwater sky.

Even the weather seems unreal on each given day,
its nature, too, transformed.

Oh there were always droughts/deluges/cold-snaps that turned cattle to statues
in Kansas, then settled in.

Once these were weather's exceptions, extremes. Now it's all extremes:
one harsh extremity after another.

All summer the forests in Oregon baked while the Pine Barrens drowned,
Europe roasting right after the deep-freeze of winter.

I imagine a parallel weather inside each day, nature still in charge.

     III

Such thoughts never entered my mind as a child, to tighten the soft, open
heart of my joy—

Then, the *cathedral forest* (the *old-growth* was) and the clear-cut
both seemed the way the world arrived,

nature before an idea to compare it to, roadless and roaded woods
     given and wondrous.

IV

"Nature:" *an idea the world cannot afford,* the thought came,
as I cut and tore blackberry runners to free some grapes.

This was true, I saw—

Wasn't it how I began to despise
all the bits of the world I thought didn't belong?

Until even the weather itself was suspect, and the sweetness seeped
out of the flavor of blackberries.

Blackberries—
                Once they were simply themselves, succulent in their syllables
their compact chambered fruit,

scribbling their tangled word over the pasture, softening
lines of the paved and mown, unsubjected to judgment.

Then I began to know "the facts": *A non-native species […] Invasive […]
aggressive […] compete for the natives' space, water and nutrients.*

No longer innocent, the blackberries, or was it me?

V

An *aesthetic nostalgia the earth cannot afford*, the thought revised itself.
        Yes, a nostalgia:

What can we know of what's best for the earth's sake except to be rid of us?

By the evidence, earth could be saying *long live the kudzu*,
English ivy, the crabgrass—all that thrives in the poorest, depleted soils.

Long live the rapid and profligate greeners, soil-anchorers, long
live the blackberry thickets where the finches took refuge in September

when the forest fell, long live the canada thistle that fed them seed all spring;
long live all the opportunistic despised, the gulls glutting themselves on the rich

rot of landfills, long live the cockroach that feeds on crumbs,
buzzards that feast on the ditch-side deer, yellowjackets that follow.

Long live the meek (which does not mean *obsequious*, which means
the undemanding ones), *who make what's discarded and given their food*
        who'll inherit the earth which will not miss the rest of us.

To love this world the way

VI

I loved my mother dying—
not despite but including her suffering—all she lost and became.

Not liking but neither resenting her thinness, her loose and wasted flesh, lively
eight-decade-old gaze she lost, the dead loose gaze the poisons replaced it with.

Sure I had preferences, the same as my mother did (her other body, another life),
but the love didn't have them,

nor was the love nostalgic for what she'd been.
Before we start, she'd told the nurse on the first day of chemo,

Before we start and I lose this, I just want you to know:
this is my own, real color!

She touched it lightly and twice, her fine dark-brown hair.
Then she sat back, relaxed, and offered up an arm.

March Vigil

It is the season of fast-dividing cells.
First the sap pressing up, then the fierce pastels.

On film, the mass looked dark and round, collapsing
star amid the astral mist of her lung.

Outside, forsythia unfurls its feathers,
the quince unclasps its fists.

The tumor is honing Mom down to essentials:
her red nails, her humor, her redred rouge.
>   (*Honey, my skin's too big. Would you
>   exchange it for me? There's a dear!*)

I fix us some lunch.
My sister arranges some blooms in a blue vase.

Mom eats, but the mass eats faster.

All night rain then more rain,

So thick it was hard to breathe.

A woman came inside
into the brick institutional

Building where we worked and lived.
She wore a wide and frightened look.

She had stepped outside
for a moment only she said

and it soaked her through.
Another came inside

with the same look saying
nothing meeting no-one's eyes.

That there could be so much
suspended up there

made us wonder
how it held

what it meant
would it stop

and what was happening
elsewhere. How wide

did the deluge stretch
we wanted to know

as though to answer the questions
would be to know.

Dawn

When the tanker tripped
over the shoal and broke,
greasing the whole sea and everything
relying on it the execs said
Oops then quarreled about blame,
exact tallies of gallons
and who was and wasn't responsible
for everything. Meanwhile

in Valdez some women who knew
what to do when you spill
began doing it, wiping the dirty
faces of murres, clearing seals'
nostrils of the mucousy blackness,
cradling each one as if it were the most
important one in the world to save,
the same way they would wash their own
children. Knowing, though no one had told them so,
how much depends on this.
Lifted, soaped even the beach
stones, their interstices like so many
toes.

And when someone thought to interview
one of the women, he asked
what did they use for the washing
and she said with authority, *"Dawn."*
Nothing else works.
"Dawn's" what we're counting on.

Spring Vigil

Rain wove its dense lead mesh over December.

Under its steady press I forgot about seasons.
That this was one, the rain persisting within it.

That the fescue would stir even so in its seed,
subject above all to light.

Then, rain's thrum and sting seemed all there was.
Weather seemed all there was. That is, the daily.

That year, spring itself preceded even the thought
of spring, and the wild forgot itself in surprise: two hawks

left off defending their ground to stand side-by-side in the field,
gazing into the first dry light.

I wasn't prepared for what I'd forgotten
even to long for:

the redwing's sudden return (little black dress,
the flutey, complicated tune).

For the hyacinths' penknives
piercing my pots of soil.

And when that bat dove past the glass at noon,
         banked,
and darted back, forth

across a certain plot of space,
over and over, a needle

darning a hole in the darkness closed, a part of me
hoped she'd succeed, whatever it cost her.

Zazen

Often, I don't think I can bear to see
what there's no stopping: the cutters

shearing their way through a hundred
acres of forest across our road,

taking down each living fir, oak and what's between,
each with its portion of cool and light,

needle-filtered and spacious; each with its shelter,
its perches and breathing which disappear

gradually, logpile by logpile, hauled
north to Longview on their way to Japan.

When I can't bear to hear anymore what I cannot
stop (not without violence) I imagine

the logs ending up in Hokkaido,
their wood nailed into zendos,

each with its portion of leaf-sieved light,
the spacious cool of its rooms, their peace,

inside of which more monks than ever will meditate,
watching their breath for the sake of all beings,

watching as violence rises and passes,
staying awake inside.

Vigils, II

She is dying in the gracious
way she does everything, today

in a turquoise linen blouse,
long nails my sister's painted *Gazpacho*.

She is so thin the Depends don't
bulge through her stylish slacks.

Now that the gastric tube's gone
from her nose, her face has lost its

cluttered look. She seems relaxed,
her expression's passed

lightly from slack to soft;
she has begun to shine.

The Bat

Bat on the asphalt,
sunlit seam of blood on one shoulder,

I want to save you,
if only from this hot, bright
dying—

and it's easy to wish it here: you
still as a stone, wings
pleated tight under you—

you seem just a tuft with tall ears
lying there, wounded
on my side of night.

But when I come to you with my catholic compassion,
bearing two sticks I would lift you oh so
tenderly up with, you will not
have it.

Dying, you force the boned, black
sails of your wings away from your sides,
stretching the great gash wide

as you strain, and fresh blood wells there.
Dying, you throw your beaked mouth
wide, and a rattled scream
tears from your throat—

> *It is the night.*
> *This is my death.*
> *You shall have none of it.*

The buzzards are coming back early from Mexico,

bringing that leisurely way they wait,
wheeling evenly over the dead and the dead-to-be.

So unlike hawks' precision spying fast mice,
their incessant tension between;

buzzards can afford to be gross and slow,
their prey in no hurry.

And what made me restive last summer
is the same as what, since, I've missed:

long, slow slide of that shadow
over the soil I've been wrestling with

all afternoon, to give in, to receive
my seed. The way it comes sometimes

in silence, sometimes making
that little tearing sound as it passes.

Moan, I

My mother is dying; she is growing
gaunt and cool. She is so done-in she can't
eat or drink or lift her tea to try;
tea which was once such pleasure, say
with a chicken salad sandwich, juicy with mayo.
Mmm! she would lean back and feign to swoon,
dabbing her mouth and re-applying her lipstick,
that tasted so good!

Now she can only lie in bed, and moan.
Little hums that start each dawn,
find their range, their rhythm, stay.
Mom, I say, do you need some more codeine?

Honey, don't worry; just let me moan.
It's so good to—I can't begin to tell you.

Deposition

The yearling hung from the fence by a tendon,
lunging and bleating.
His snagged leg had twisted about
off its hoof, and the hoof
snapped and flipped like a rabbit's foot
strung on a chain each time he pushed off,
pushed off again.

Tarmac simmered in the sun where we stood, uncertain.
The vineyard wavered in the vapors.

And I tell you I wanted to run from, not to him—

But we were *it* that day, the only ones there,
and he was bleating and lunging so explicitly toward us—

So, while my love pried his gristle and hide
from the wire, I held the whole hanging rest of the body
to keep him still.

It took forever.

All was shudder and bawl as I heard myself
start to chant:
      sorry sorry sorry
I sang, to keep holding...

Then, when his leg tore loose and he fell
to the grass all still but his sides—little bellows—
heaving and caving; when we saw

we'd have to kill him and couldn't—
while we couldn't we held him until we could,
then while he jerked, arched, died...

until the syrupy blood of him cooled
and stilled we held him—Christ knows
how long we stayed and held him,
or what a difference it made.

Vigils, IV

After her last, real breath
and reflexive gasps that follow,

when she is fully still I lie
down and long beside her,

wrapping my body around what she couldn't
help holding back in life: her body.

All my life she'd been so jumpy;
snuggling, you'd think you'd hit her
breast with a stone.

Now she is relaxed, and I can be with her
like this a little, skin pressed
close and still.

As though I'd been lifted out, then been laid
down again beside her, as a separate being,

to receive, to begin to live
with longing—

before standing up,
I lie down.

My Mother's Teeth

Before the men came for the body
I lay down beside her one final time.

Lay down the length of her,
molding my flesh to her cooling frame.

Then I lifted her teeth from their glass,
slid them back inside.

And it shocked me a little, how intimate this felt;
more than washing the violet folds of her vulva,

changing the bandage that covered her bedsore,
tracing the paths of her chemo-scarred veins.

Inside, her mouth was hard, unyielding,
cool as the metal bowl she'd used whipping up

cream, shelling peas; song of those peas on steel
frank as her speech had been.

Words she'd loved, shocked, admonished
my world with had come from this mouth

which my fingers were inside now,
fumbling inside the dark slick of it,

determined, before the men came,
to make them fit, put her bite back

in the body where it belonged,
where I'd know how to find it.

To September

Now the valley's all bees and pears and crisp grass.

Sun's left its perch to lie low all day with shadows.
Poplars disperse all the gold they've saved.

Above, in the fastnesses,
old ice dissolves and slides down,

joining, informing the river's muscle of silk, steel,
glass the salmon will their way up through.

All this ferocious surrender!
All those husks and juice!

How the caddis flies break from their cases, sip,
and the dying salmon rise—

The Change (My Mother Has the Last Word)

Oak leaves yellow in a single turn.
They were brownish yesterday—changed

overnight to their dusty, brassy dresses—
old, painted stripes on a country road,
Palmolive liquid, its heavy, lurid glow.

Still between stormy spells, water ticking off trees.

Seems like it's all over now but "the symptoms":
aching and sleeplessness, heart unexpectedly
pounding against my chest,

unexpectedly settling down.

Did I mention the aching?
As though every sinew, each muscle and cell
strains to tear itself free, to escape the body.

Last night I woke three times in the throes of dread.

A dream organized itself around each spell,
making a focused and shapely anxiety.

In one dream, there's a break-in. I'm trapped
in my room; the dark crackles with malice.

In one, the friend who never calls
except to announce the death of some other friend
drops over, setting off my dread.

The angel of death, he seems
this time, *come for me*.

Meanwhile and all night, the warm, wet
storm: squalls, then some spells of still.

This year, for the first time, I added red to my hair.
Not to cover—to keep the grey company.

Dead mom, what was this like for you? *Oh honey,
I don't know—I really don't remember.*

*If you don't make a big deal of it though
it won't be a big deal.*

On Meaning

A desperation for form drew me to the page.

Not that I knew; I only knew despair,
drawn to the page.

Some words went down, circled
and composed themselves.

Making a small music,
a narrow wedge of light.

Which did not cure, but warmed.

Huis Clos

I walked on the wet moor, wept over Mom.

This was after the chatter of sidewalk shoes
in the city (any city but it may have been
San Francisco) where I went to shop.

A skirt-and-cardigans shop, it was
woolly with sweater-coats. I'd looked

forward to browsing but a shopper accosted me.
Warmly, but accosted me, a stranger,

to help her choose. These shoes or
those with this nest of skirts.
The skirts wore prints and frills.

She flipped them back on their rack
like the leaves of books, lifted a beige

open-toed pump to the assembled
clothes, and I nodded uncertainly.

I wear neutrals with everything,
I said, *but that may not be you.*

Long, vivid, cardigan sweater-and-skirt displays
festooned the walls.

          I turned—
a bulky muscular woman inside a red
dress with a hat to match started up talking.

Her face was ruddy, thick-textured;
I remember its wide, deep pores.

Appears anxious, w/marked speech pressure,
no dysfluencies, somewhat tangential. Thought
content w/o delusions or formal disorder. Eye
contact intermittent, psychomotor WNL

—this came unbidden to mind.
Then, that she was male.

Now I no longer wanted to shop at all—
I was hungry,
very suddenly hungry, now.

Down the street, where the sidewalk ended
in sand and a mist-thick hint of hills,
a Chinese restaurant added its humid,
chickeny breath to the silky breeze.

The walls were open; inside a table of diners
urged me *(sit down, sit down!)* to join them—
how could I say no?

I was handed a menu, but the man at the head
had just finished the ordering; hot shrimp,

steaming dim sum in bowls were already
arriving. His menu closed, then mine.

After a long hike,

went to the park and sat down awhile.

Half-listened to jazz there,
staring at a square of crisp grass.

Into which a bumblebee stumbled,
dogged and hurrying.

Listing, righting itself, it
lugged itself up each bent-blade

hill then lumbered down again,
and never veered or flagged,

keeping this fierce, impossible
pace, that aim.

Heaving the body's bulk
ahead on thready legs,

making a beeline nowhere I could
imagine, somewhere it couldn't see.

Moving the way a creature meant to fly
would move, who thought its legs could get it there.

Imaging

I kept my gaze aimed high.
Slipped off the black silk brassiere
I'd arrived in,
slipped on the gingham gown.

Which was white,
flowered with that crafty hospital blue
that ratchets up my fears,
devised as it is to soothe.

So we scare you now? My breasts
would accuse if I looked their way,
my having hauled them in here to Imaging
like carry-on bags that might contain a bomb.

Having answered the questions:
"Do you have silicone implants?"
      (Did you pack all your bags yourself?)
"Are your nipples retracted? If so,
for how many days___? Weeks___? Months___?"
      (Have your bags been out of your
      sight at any time since you arrived?)

No, they've always been with me...

That I'm just following orders
not to trust any breasts over thirty
(*nothing personal–*) wouldn't fly.

Of course it was personal, the idea itself
had already divided us, *them* from *me*.
It is the first loss, that fissure.
Then, the suspicions.

And that night I dream I'm stopped at a light,
about to drive off when this guy runs
up out of nowhere, opens my trunk,
slips something small inside. He doesn't
say, but I know it's a timed explosive,
enough to blow my life to bits, and any
lives nearby. Maybe in the next second,
maybe hours or days from now,
who knows?

And the odd thing is, I don't stop,
don't even peek in the trunk.
I know and just keep driving.

And Rise

I lay down, I became unmade.

Left the garden gate open, let the deer come help themselves
    and go.

Let the high apples and last blackberries fall—
    never gathered these.

Fasted, not as an act of will, but from some inner refusal.

Could not know if this *no* would cleanse or kill—either way
helpless to refuse the refusal.

Let the frantic heart flutter against its walls,
a swallow trapped in the eaves.

Was so cold—layered clothes upon clothes as though inside a cold
    shade the exact size of the self, even as mists dispersed
    from the field and chrysanthemums grew thirsty in clay pots
    under the September sun, the cat purring outside in a gold pool—

woke at night in a sweat to go cold again.

Knew a small and pleasureless peace sitting still in a room, the heart
stilled for a spell setting words on a page, as now.

Felt unable and sourceless.
Could not imagine otherwise.

Slept and rose, sank and rose for days, as the arm of a pump works without
    expectation above the unseen, the unknown well, its vacuum
    sucking up empty space over and over, until without warning
    a dribble with rust appears
    and then a rush, clear.

Riparian Zone Restoration Plan

I want to plant an *ash swale* its words say
water sloshing around in a pail a splash a

swath in the pasture soaking the silty
loam where trees will rise as whispers.

First Day of Autumn

No wind, and not much discernibly moved
as I walked up the road,

so that change in its essence was visible; no dramas
of action, resistance (the curled leaf skidding across asphalt).

Maples stood still in their turning, leaves yellow-green to brown.
Mist gathered and dispersed from the fields in translucent gestures.

Still shapely, blackberries hovered between ripeness and rot.
        I picked one—
it dissolved in my fingers.

Beyond the last curve toward home,
the clear-cut appeared, for once

not what I'd seen since the trees went down (a ghostly
absence of forest), but what it was:

a bright and brushy hill, lovely in its way
not mine.

The Stonefly

Each year, hiking the Bagby trail up
to the hotsprings, crossing the cedar log
bridging the Callowash, I'd loosen

the carapace made of my worries
       & let it drop
into the flow & stones.

There'd be other new worries ahead
but they wouldn't be those ones.

Still Life with Conifers
(Timberline, Oregon, July 2008)

Trees tip downhill through old slabs of snow.
They look stunned and flayed.

Three cedars lean onto a thatch of pines;
siskins flit through like nurses' aides.

      Such a long, sealed-in spell under such a load—

Is it me, or are they unsure what to do, the trees,
stiff fronds resisting the breeze
so newly free?

The Eddy Fence

Rush Creek Point Lookout, the Idaho Rockies,
our just-married summer, 1975.

The high-flung, spectacular peaks and the solitude
just as we dreamed these, as well as nothing-like.

The way the rose, gold high-altitude sunlight
fell through east-facing windows at five a.m.,
making a hothouse.

At six, the fire radio's crackle just before the voice,
first noise of the day from the distant rim of the fastnesses.

Ring of the axe through the high, thin air,
clang of cast iron pans—

how these glanced off, without breaking, the silence.

Silence a glacial pool, clean and transparent.
Tensile, a matrix of light and rock.

We took turns hauling water-bags up from the distant spring,

crossing the bee-singing, hyssopy sidehill,
braving the thirsts of the rustling copse.

And always the watching, the watching for smoke,

scanning the visible world with binoculars, spying
on granite and stands of pine, shimmering
auras that outlined their images.

At night in a lightning storm
            (oh the charge and *frisson* of it,
                all that the gratuitous *son et lumière*!)
we tracked strikes on the map with tacks; later
scanned for wisps in the mist-ghosted dawn.

All summer, no one made the eighty-mile,
gravel-road drive from McCall to the trail,

then the three-day hike to our peak—
it was too hard and far.

What we'd dreamed of, this also was.

        How your solitude loved it there,
loved me in mine.

■ ■ ■

Still, while we had it, I could not... what?
Bear it, I guess: what I'd wanted.

        In the pictures I'm happy.
In the pictures we're beautiful,

            smiling and spare and tanned,
            strong as the landscape upsweeping us.

What frightened me: not the lightning,
not the black bear that sometimes appeared at the spring—

What frightened: all that terrible beauty's insistence
and inescape.

That it was stronger than I was.
                              Would change me,
with or without my permission.

All summer, resisting, I made myself miserable.
Resisting, hating my fear.

Fear (and my fighting-with) keeping me separate.
Fear (and my fighting-with) a form of refusal
I could not, yet, refuse.

■ ■ ■

You, disappearing—

Something began to unreel like a spool as you tromped
down the trail. To unwind like a fishing line caught on your shoe,

I could almost see it, this filament, as the trees took you in.
Something I guess I had given (when?)
which went with you now; which you now, evidently

were taking. Whatever it is that receives,
digests sustenance, leaving me.

I turned back to the dishes. Dusklight and dishwater
sluiced over my hands, rinsing
your disappearance not off, but into them.

I ate a handful of raisins.
They tasted like sand.

In the days that followed, only in motion
were shreds of ease, and moving was what I did,
chopping & sweeping & hauling & stoking & sawing
& scraping & stacking & kneading & scrubbing
& scanning—
only then would the heart's heavy beat disappear,
into motion, its element, mute & perpetual.

I suppose I slept, but I can't remember the rest of it.

■ ■ ■

Nostalgia:

Not a longing for what was loved and lost.
I thought this was it, but it isn't.

Regret, yes. Desire? Yes.
But not for any earlier, more-loved times.

For the opposite:
all I couldn't receive when it came to me.

Could not entirely,
not in proportion.

The full, entire happinesses of life so far:
those I've mostly forgotten.

Oh, I can recall them, but they don't persist,
stirring up longing—

to remember joy is to renew delight.
       Fleeting, as is its nature (delight's),
but untinged: nothing kept apart from the body
for missing to stick onto.

Sweetness refused is that alien irritant:
grit which the missing adheres to, surrounds.

Nostalgia's its sorrow, a species of wistfulness
for all the joys missed, not the ones received.

We all want more intimacy than we can tolerate,
a teacher said to me years ago.

I was young, but I apprehended right away.
(Oh, apprehension: the sudden seeing-a-whole,

then the long, slow slog that follows,
to understand!)

■ ■ ■

On the river one day, love, you showed me an eddy fence.

See where some current slides left into backwater?
How it slows and pools while the rest keeps on rushing?

As though the water'd divided and stayed still whole:
one water, two ways, the fence its shift and glue,

itself nothing, the water—a hundred percent of it—
backing or flowing, nothing left for the fence,

yet there the fence was, non-existing in spite of this.

And where you find one you fish it, you'd showed me then.
See all the matter that catches there?
And I saw:

insect shells seed cases
twigs and some clots of foam
dust in a rusty scum.
Fragile steeples of mayflies' wings transparent in sunlight.

All these bits of the living and fallen dead
matted lightly together there,
felting a rind, a seam.

Locating the fence and adorning it,
yet not, of themselves, the fence.

Saw a trout sipping, passing with ease
between regions of swirl and flow which the eddy fence was.

Not a dwelling I saw
a way.

Moan, II

A waitress is eating her lunch while the other serves.
Slim and chic in her tight black slacks, black stylish
shoes, she eats with her back to us, something
molten and toasted, fragrant with soft, strong cheese.
She is reading the paper, and as she chews
these little moans begin, rising from somewhere
rich and deep inside to sing through her
nose. *Mmm!* She hums,
chews and hum-sighs again, *Mm-ah-Mm!*
She is in a kind of trance—she does not hear
herself, her body noisy with praise,
with the sweetness of all it's receiving, the body
humming without her permission, sliding down
little three-tone trills of sound, their vibrations
turning her slightly transparent as she studies
the news, beside herself with joy.

The Undoing

I hadn't thought about
what it would be like—hadn't even
wondered—

only what it wouldn't, I hoped,
be anymore: my father's ghost-gaze
over the bed,

sucking dry first
my pleasure, later
even the idea of pleasure.

And the panics—strange fires—
maybe these would pass.

The world outside was like that:
the world, outside.
A sort of mural, the true

world, I assumed, behind it,
all The Answers shining
inside, a bright library.

I hoped something different would happen,
waited.

And when it began
to happen it wasn't different
exactly—wasn't *like* anything
I thought. It wasn't thought.

Was in *things*: rush of joy in my bowels
at the snort and crash of deer in the brush
at dusk. The way the moon

rising a sliver short of full one night
slipped behind my face and shone
back at itself from there and kept on

shining. In the scents of summer:
blackberries. Dust. Straw. The secret
odors of creekbeds. What had been

detached from the source now reeled
out from it, threading me

nostril to groin, then tugged
back toward the four winds
sweetly undoing me.

Now when I climb the stairs
to my room,

when I close my eyes and call
the beloved the beloved
comes to me, a blue shadow

delicate, fluid, becoming the whole
curve of my arms, my fingers'
lacings-together, every unthought
desire, its answer.

And the dreams: sure,
sometimes I still find myself
trapped in the lift soaring out of control
past the numbered floors,
but more often

broad waters glisten to receive me.
I hesitate, slip in
and am upheld—

Acknowledgements

Grateful acknowledgement is made to editors of the periodicals and anthologies in which versions of the following poems first appeared:

Calyx: "Standard Time"
Christian Century: "Between" and "The Bat"
A Fine Madness: "First Ice"
High Desert Journal: "The buzzards are coming back early from Mexico,"
The Dunes Review: "Blackberries"
Yes (Anthology from the Silverton Poetry Festival): "The Sanctuary"
Gaia: "Dawn"
Fireweed: "View of Mt. St. Helens at the End of a Love Affair"
Tcha Teemanwi: Poems of Mary's Peak (Anthology): "To September"

A few of the poems in this book first appeared, in earlier versions, in one or another of the following chapbooks: *Transparent Woman*, Howlet Press, 2006; and *Gazpacho* (with Darcy V. Henderson), Two Sisters Press, 2001.

Many thanks to those mentors and editors who were of particular help in this collection's development: Carter McKenzie, Anita Sullivan, Jessica Lamb, Eleanor Wilner, Karen Brennan, and Joan Aleshire.

Thanks also to Chase Twichell, Amy Grimm, and the Squaw Valley Community of Writers for their repeated and persistent support.

Colophon

Titles are set in Futura Light, with poetry text set in Goudy Old Style.

Typeset by ImPrint Services, Corvallis, Oregon.